I0458935

Ruth's Need for
a Redeemer

Ruth's Need for a Redeemer

A Bible Study on Loss, Loyalty, and Unexpected Love

Plano, Texas

Ruth's Need for a Redeemer: A Bible Study on Loss, Loyalty, and Unexpected Love

Copyright © 2025 by Stephanie Watson

All rights reserved.

No part of this work may be reproduced or transmitted in any form or by any means, electronic or mechanical, including photocopying and recording, or by any information storage or retrieval system, except as may be expressly permitted by the 1976 Copyright Act or in writing from the publisher. Requests for permission can be addressed to Permissions, Invite Press, P.O. Box 260917, Plano, TX 75026.

This book is printed on acid-free, elemental chlorine-free paper.

ISBN: Paperback: 978-1-963265-64-4

All Scripture quotations unless noted otherwise are taken from the Holy Bible, New International Version®, NIV® Copyright ©1973, 1978, 1984, 2011 by Biblica, Inc.™ Used by permission of Zondervan. All rights reserved worldwide.

Scripture quotations marked NKJV are from The Holy Bible, New King James Version, Copyright © 1982 by Thomas Nelson. Used by permission. All rights reserved.

Scripture quotations marked NET are from the NET Bible® copyright © 1996, 2019 by Biblical Studies Press, L.L.C. http://netbible.com All rights reserved.

Scripture quotations marked NASB are from the New American Standard Bible, Copyright © 1960. 1962, 1963, 1968, 1971, 1972, 1973, 1975, 1977, 1995, 2020 by The Lockman Foundation. All rights reserved. Used by permission. (www.Lockman.org)

25 26 27 28 29 30 31 32 33 34—10 9 8 7 6 5 4 3 2 1

MANUFACTURED IN THE UNITED STATES OF AMERICA

CONTENTS

WELCOME LETTER

Dear Reader,

Wherever you are, whatever you are going through, the fact that you hold this book in your hands is no accident. You are an answer to prayer. Let me tell you why.

The Table ministry was created to nourish women spiritually through bite-size, approachable Bible studies. Whether you have studied the Bible for years or are opening it for the first time, The Table Bible Studies are designed for you.

My name is Stephanie Watson; I had the honor and privilege of writing the words in this Bible study. The journey of writing and teaching is a road I never in my wildest dreams imagined traveling. If you and I were to sit down for a cup of coffee to get to know one another, I would tell you how much I love sightseeing all over the world with my husband, that my favorite evenings are savoring the conversation and antics of my growing kids around the dinner table, and the joy that it brings me when I get a chance to spend the day laughing with my friends. I would also undoubtedly tell you the reason that I write is because I fell in love with the Lord through Bible study, and I desire for you to receive that same gift God gave me.

I grew up in a family who took me to church every Sunday. I specifically remember the moment in my grandparents' home when I accepted Jesus as my Savior. I knew that Jesus loved me, but I didn't realize I needed anything beyond church on Sundays and my occasional prayers at mealtime and bedtime. I was satisfied with my faith until God intervened and worked a miracle that changed everything.

My miracle came through the gift of gathering around a table with a small group of women who opened the Bible, read it, and then engaged in honest conversations about Scripture. It was a miracle in the simplest yet most profound form. I can still remember those early discussions around that table. I would listen as they reflected on Scripture and spoke of God. I was amazed they could laugh over quirky stories in the Old Testament and share details of the life of Jesus that I had never known existed. Reading and soaking in the moments around the table made me realize that God was so much bigger, more significant, and more powerful than I had ever imagined.

The Bible isn't just a big, boring book; it is filled with real people facing real problems, and behind every one of them is a God full of unfailing love who is working for their good! This is what I needed to know. The same God of the Bible is the same God who is working in my life today. Through my weekly gatherings with faith-filled women, I realized I didn't just need God on Sunday mornings; I desperately needed Him every moment of every day.

Once I got started studying Scripture, my hunger for the Lord grew in unimaginable ways. God unlocked a key to my heart that I didn't know needed to be accessed, but once the door was open, I could feel God working in my life each and every day. This was the greatest gift He could have given me. While I call this a miracle in my life, the reality is this is a gift that God offers each of us. God wrote the Bible to reveal Himself to us. He desires for us to read His message. He desires for us to talk about it with others. The

Bible is the gift God gave all generations so that no matter where we are, no matter what we are going through, we can open it and hear His voice speaking over our lives.

Before we began The Table studies, we prayed that the Lord would prepare a seat at The Table for every woman. We prayed that The Table would transform women, families, and generations. You are an answer to prayer because we prayed you would know that this study is prepared for you. God already knew your name. He prepared your seat for you to come to know your Savior and Redeemer in a new and personal way.

Most of all, we pray that through this study, you would "Taste and see that the LORD is good!" (Psalm 34:8). So, pull up your seat, grab a cup of coffee, and find someone to chat with.

Your Table gal,
Stephanie

THE REDEEMER STUDY SERIES

Welcome to *Ruth's Need for a Redeemer* study, part one of a three-part series on how God used the extraordinary faith of women to bring redemption to the world.

The more I study Scripture, the more humbled I am by how great our God is and how powerful a storyteller He is. One of the profound revelations I have experienced is understanding that every detailed story in the Bible connects to tell one unified narrative. Like scenes in a movie, each story and character within the Bible builds upon the previous one. Just as you need to understand what happens at a movie's beginning to give meaning to the middle and the ending, the same applies to the Bible.

The thread of redemption runs through the biblical narrative from the moment of Adam and Eve's first sin in Genesis to the new creation of Heaven and Earth at the end of Revelation. Redemption means "an act or the state of being rescued."* Through the Bible, God reveals that we desperately need to be rescued from the brokenness within ourselves and in this world. Redemption is not possible to achieve on our own. We cannot rescue ourselves; God is the one who did and is doing the rescue by paying the necessary ransom for redemption. Jesus is the Redeemer that each and every one of us needs.

––––––––––––––––

* Dictionary.com, 2025.

The Redeemer series explores the women in Scripture as an integral part of the redemption story.

Study 1: *Ruth's Need for a Redeemer*
Study 2: *Hannah and Mary's Trust in the Redeemer*
Study 3: *The Women of the Gospels' Life with the Redeemer*

These women, spanning the Old Testament to the New Testament, demonstrate extraordinary faith to be bold enough to proclaim, trust in, and live their lives redeemed. Their example of faith teaches us why we need a redeemer, how to fully trust the redeemer, and how to live daily with the redeemer.

Ruth's Need for a Redeemer study will examine the life of Ruth in the Old Testament. Ruth was a foreigner, a childless widow, and considered an outcast among God's people. Her future appeared bleak and hopeless to all around her, but against all odds, her loyal faith guided her path. Ruth's life is an example of everyday faith, placing one step in front of the other. Her story is a powerful redemption story.

INTRODUCTION

WHAT TO EXPECT

Ruth's Need for a Redeemer study will walk you verse by verse through the book of Ruth. Each weekly lesson includes a three-part sequence:

1. Personal Bible Study Scripture and Questions to complete independently throughout the week (~1 hour of study per week). Each lesson includes:
   - Scripture passage from the NIV translation. Additional Scripture references connected to the central passage are provided at the end of each weekly lesson.
   - Reflect and respond to questions that correspond to the Scripture passage.
   - Pray the Psalm located at the end of your lesson as you complete your personal study. Reflect on the Psalm throughout the week as you draw near to the Lord.
2. Meet with your Table Small Group to discuss the Scripture and questions that you answered in your independent study time.
3. Watch the teaching video to deepen and solidify your learning of the lesson that you studied and discussed with your group.
   - Notes pages are included for each video teaching session.

As you go through each weekly lesson, I want you to understand the benefits of studying in this sequence. Studies show that the average audience listening to a teaching or sermon remembers only 5% of what they hear. If you skip to step 3 and watch the teaching video without doing steps 1 and 2, then the impact it will have on you is very small. The good news is that studies show when people engage in conversations about a topic, they typically retain 50% of that discussion. This is why attending and actively participating in group discussions is so important. The better news is if you interact with the Scripture by reading, contemplating, and answering questions before the discussion or listening to the teaching, you will remember significantly more. Having already thought about the passage and processed it, your brain can retain the info from video teachings! That is when they will have the most significant impact on your life! But there is one more kicker. After doing steps 1, 2, and 3, if you share what you've learned with someone else, then you are teaching. When you teach, you retain 90% of that information!* Isn't that great?

Savor the story of Ruth. Reflect on what happened in her life. Answer the questions to help you recognize how Ruth's example relates to your life. Participate in your table discussions. Use your voice. The act of sharing what you've learned is important! Then, engage while listening to the teaching. You have note pages to keep your thoughts fresh and to remember the details that resonate with you. Appreciate each aspect of it. Finally, go and share at least one thing from each lesson with someone in your life. This will solidify the time you spend studying. You don't want to forget what God is teaching you, and you shouldn't keep it to yourself. Share the extraordinary faith of Ruth with others!

---

* Adapted from the NTL Institute of Applied Behavioral Science Learning Pyramid.

The most important thing to remember is that the goal of all this is to know the God who created you, who deeply loves you, and who came to redeem you. Not every week of your study will be perfect, but God is not looking for perfection. What He desires is your heart. If you come to the study and can only complete one or two steps that week, that is absolutely okay! Doing a little bit, or even just reading the Scripture, is a step in your journey and a significant one at that. If you have an off week, I encourage you to keep going. Come back the next week. Don't give up! God loves every aspect of who you are and is with you every moment of your journey.

WHAT TO STUDY EACH WEEK

Personal study preparation before your discussion and video viewing:

Before week 1: No preparation needed
Before week 2: Complete week 2 reading and study questions
Before week 3: Complete week 3 reading and study questions
Before week 4: Complete week 4 reading and study questions
Before week 5: Complete week 5 reading and study questions
Before week 6: Complete week 6 reading and study questions
Before week 7: Complete week 7 reading and study questions

PARTICIPATING AS AN INDIVIDUAL

If you are studying this on your own, wonderful! God has so much to teach you in the book of Ruth! I am thrilled that you are here. Each week do the three-step process outlined in the *What to Expect* section above. For step 2, the discussion portion, I encourage you to get creative. Find anyone who you could talk to about what you are learning. A friend, a family member, a neighbor, a child, or anyone who would listen. Quite possibly, if you find someone to talk to they might want to jump in on this journey with you. Or, each week, find someone new to talk to, you never know who God might lead you to share a small tidbit with. This is your adventure! My most significant encouragement is not to rush through the study. Savor it! Take time in your personal study to think through and pray about the questions before you jump into watching the video. The more you wrestle with the Scripture, the more it will stick with you. After you have completed your weekly lesson, write down at least one big takeaway that you want to remember and apply in your life.

THE TABLE GROUP MEETING SCHEDULE FORMAT

If you are working through this study as a group, plan a weekly group meeting for the seven weeks of the study. Set a day of the week that works for everyone. You should plan for your gatherings to last around an hour and a half. This will include time to discuss your lesson and then watch the teaching video together.

Weekly Table Gathering example schedule:

> Gathering & Fellowship (10 minutes)
> Leader led welcome & opening prayer (5 minutes)
> Break into small group discussions of about 10–12 people led by one table leader (40 minutes)
> Read through provided weekly Scripture
> Discussion of provided weekly personal study questions
> See notes for Table Leaders section below
> Watch provided teaching video as a large group (35 minutes)
> Leader led closing remarks and make sure everyone has all they need for next week

The Table Best Practices

Come Prepared

- Bring your study, Bible, and pen
- Silence your cell phone

Build Connections

- Listen with genuine care
- Express differing opinions without a critical tone
- Be trustworthy with what is shared by others

Table Talk

- New things learned from the Bible
- Transparent, honest conversation
- Freedom to express doubts and struggles
- Balanced sharing allows everyone to participate

Off the Table

- Avoid any conversations that cause division
- Avoid politics, denominations/pastors, celebrities, gossip, etc.

Notes for Table Group Leaders

Hi Table Leaders! Thank you for saying "yes" to this essential role at The Table. We are praying for you in all that you do. One thing I deeply desire for you to know is that you do not need to be a Bible scholar or feel like you have every part of your life figured out. The only thing that you need is faith in our Lord Jesus Christ. That simple act of believing means that you will allow the Lord to lead, trusting God each step of the way.

We see The Table discussion as when Bible study comes to life! Through the conversations around your table, relationships will be built. Friendships and community will form in unexpected ways. These conversations and connections will keep your women coming back for more. Good discussions allow women to mature in their faith and learn to not only say they are Christians but also understand how to live out their faith.

Are you ready to embark on this journey? Here are some tips and tricks to get you started. But first and foremost, pray every step of the way. The Lord is the one who is doing the work through you.

Before Your First Week

- Pray for the Lord to begin making connections at your Table before you even begin.
- Reach out to the women in your Table Group, welcoming them to your Table.
- Make sure each woman has their own study materials.
- Create place cards or nametags before the women arrive.

Group Discussion Dynamics

The goal of discussion is for the women to grow in their understanding of God through conversation about Scripture.

As a Table Leader, your role is to guide the discussion. You do not need to teach nor should you dominate the conversation. As a leader, you have the privilege of steering the conversation, keeping it focused on knowing God more.

Keep the following in mind as you lead your discussion:

- Ask the provided questions for that week's lesson.
- If time allows, read the Scripture together.

- Share occasionally to spur on conversation but limit your sharing.
  - Warning: the more you share, the more the group will look to you for the answers and not share themselves
- Try to keep sharing balanced among the women in the group.
- Don't be afraid of silence.
  - Some groups need time to think about their answers or to find the courage to speak. Allow them the time. The silence feels forever to the leader, but it is an opportunity for the Lord to speak through someone else. Let them break the silence instead of you.
  - Ask the question differently or in your own words if the women do not understand.
  - Direct them to the Scripture passage to spur on the conversation.
- Resist the urge to offer advice.
  - Let your women encourage each other.
- Do not directly call out the quiet women in your group. Instead, let the group know that you would like to hear from someone who hasn't shared yet. If they choose not to share, that is okay. Allow them the opportunity to speak when they are ready, but listening might be all they feel up to that week.
- Move the discussion along to not get stuck on one topic or one person.
  - If the discussion has gone down a rabbit trail that has taken the entire group off track, redirect the conversation to the Scripture and lesson questions.
  - Women will get frustrated and stop coming if the conversation is continually off-topic.
- Pray for the Holy Spirit to guide your conversation.

God is with you at your Table! You are not alone in this role. Trust Him in your discussions. You will be amazed at how He reveals Himself to you and your women.

COMPANION TEACHING VIDEOS

This workbook includes access to seven teaching videos, one for each session of *Ruth's Need for a Redeemer* by Stephanie Watson.

Each video is designed to be watched together at the end of your group's meeting to deepen and solidify your learning of the lesson that you studied and discussed.

HOW TO WATCH

Scan the QR Code below or visit

https://www.inviteministries.org/ruths-need

IF PROMPTED, ENTER THE ACCESS CODE:

aodkr.lzm18

That's it! Each session's video will appear on the page.

Tip for Leaders: Preview the video before your group meets.

Need help? Email info@InviteMinistries.org

These videos are a free supplement for workbook buyers.

RUTH'S NEED FOR A REDEEMER

Ruth, the outsider, needs a redeemer
to be secure in God's promises

Week 1
GOD'S REDEMPTION PLAN

The Book of Ruth is a beautiful and unique story in the Bible. Most stories of people in the Old Testament follow the lineage of the descendants of Abraham, through whom God promised to build the nation of Israel. Ruth did not follow that pattern. She was not born in Israel; she was a pagan woman from the despised country of Moab, who married into an Israelite family. At first glance, it would seem as though her short four-chapter book, tucked between the books of Judges and Samuel in the Old Testament, is just a sweet love story. You might even skim through it, thinking it pales in comparison to the other stories that tell the lives of the powerful patriarchs like Abraham, Isaac, Jacob, Joseph, Judah, Moses, and King David. But in reality, Ruth's faith in God played a pivotal role in fulfilling God's promises to the patriarchs. Ruth's unexpected story connects the dots from God's promises to Abraham to King David and our Redeemer Jesus. The life of Ruth is not a story we should skim through but one to dive into and get to know her.

Before we get to know Ruth, take some time to get to know the women who are embarking on this study with you. Go around the table and share a little about yourself, then answer the icebreaker question: What is one of your favorite books or movies and why?

LEARN

Talking about movies and books is fun! We all love to cozy up by the fireplace with a great book or to pop popcorn and gather around to watch a movie because everyone loves a good story. The Bible is also a story. From beginning to end, God masterfully wrote the greatest story ever told. When we open the Bible, we get to hear God speaking directly to us, telling us His redemption story.

Read a snippet of the redemption promises that God made in the following Scriptures, then discuss as a group the questions provided.

In Genesis 12, the Lord came to Abraham to make a promise to him. Read this promise:

Genesis 12:1–3

[1] The LORD had said to Abram, "Go from your country, your people and your father's household to the land I will show you.
[2] "I will make you into a great nation, and I will bless you;
I will make your name great, and you will be a blessing.
[3] I will bless those who bless you, and whoever curses you I will curse;
and all peoples on earth will be blessed through you."

What did God promise He would do for Abraham?

....
....
....
....
....
....
....
....
....

Who does God say will be blessed through Abraham?

....
....
....
....
....
....
....
....
....

Does God give any stipulation that could lead to breaking this promise He made to Abraham?

In 2 Samuel 7, God comes to make another promise. This time, God makes a promise to King David. Read a portion of this promise below:

READ
2 Samuel 7:8–9, 16

....

8 "Now then, tell my servant David, 'This is what the LORD Almighty says: I took you from the pasture, from tending the flock, and appointed you ruler over my people Israel. 9 I have been with you wherever you have gone, and I have cut off all your enemies from before you. Now I will make your name great, like the names of the greatest men on earth.

16 Your house and your kingdom will endure forever before me; your throne will be established forever.'"

What did God reveal He had already done in David's life?

....
....
....
....
....
....
....
....
....
....

What did God promise to do for David in the future?

How might we be blessed through God's promises to Abraham and David?

Ruth's story and life came between these two declarations from God. Scholars estimate Ruth lived around 800–900 years after Abraham and 60–100 years before King David*. Over the 1,000-year time span between these two declarations, God was at work to fulfill the promises He made. He is still at work today. Throughout the weeks of this study, we will revisit these passages to see how Ruth's life is connected to God's promises.

> Play the teaching video for Week One. Use the NOTES page to take notes on anything that stands out to you.
> See page 8 for video access instructions.

---

* Eugene H. Merrill, *Kingdom of Priests*, p. 47, 261; Dr. Thomas L. Constable, "Notes on Ruth," 2024 Edition, soniclight.com, p. 3.

NOTES

Week 2
THE PATH OF DEVASTATION

Welcome to the beginning of Ruth's story! This week, as you study, you will be introduced to the time period of Israel in which Ruth lived. It was a time when issues and struggles as a nation were evident, and the main characters of the story were in the midst of tragedy. The first verses of the Book of Ruth introduce you to a woman named Naomi, her family, and the circumstances that led her son to marry Ruth the Moabite. At the end of this week's reading, Ruth and Naomi's lives appear bleak, and devastation engulfs them. Their all-encompassing heartbreak darkens the lens of possible redemption.

As you read their story, consider your own—a time when you experienced suffering and couldn't imagine how God would redeem your story. How and when did God redeem that experience? Or are you still waiting for Him to? Either way, the story of Ruth can speak to that moment in your life. As you watch these women struggle, wait, and witness the Lord at work in their lives, remember that the God who cared deeply for Naomi and Ruth is the same God who loves and cares for you.

Spend time this week reading through the provided Scripture and answering the coinciding questions. The questions do not have right or wrong answers; they are simply to get you thinking. Enjoy your time with God. When you gather as a group, discuss the questions. Share with each other what you are learning. Savor the discussion around "The Table." Once you have discussed all the questions, play the teaching video for Week 2.

LEARN

The Book of Ruth takes place during the time of the Judges in Israel (approx. 1370–1050 BC)*. This was after the Israelites had escaped slavery in Egypt under Moses' leadership. They had wandered in the desert for 40 years, and then Joshua led the nation of Israel into the promised land. It is called the promised land because it is the land that God promised Abraham that his descendants would inhabit in Genesis 12:1–3. Prior to Israel receiving the gift of living in the promised land, God spoke His commandments to the nation for them to be sure to remember.

---

* Carl G. Rasmussen, *Zondervan Atlas of the Bible* (Grand Rapids, MI: Zondervan, 2010), p. 121.

READ
Deuteronomy 6:3–7, 12

³ Hear, Israel, and be careful to obey so that it may go well with you and that you may increase greatly in a land flowing with milk and honey, just as the Lord, the God of your ancestors, promised you.

⁴ Hear, O Israel: The Lord our God, the Lord is one. ⁵ Love the Lord your God with all your heart and with all your soul and with all your strength. ⁶ These commandments that I give you today are to be on your hearts. ⁷ Impress them on your children. Talk about them when you sit at home and when you walk along the road, when you lie down and when you get up.

¹² be careful that you do not forget the Lord, who brought you out of Egypt, out of the land of slavery.

According to verses 4–5, what did God desire from the Israelites?

Verse 12 warns the Israelites to *be careful not to forget the Lord*. How might verse 7 help them to remember the Lord always?

....
....
....
....
....
....
....
....
....
....
....
....
....
....
....
....
....
....

The generation who entered the promised land served the Lord well under Joshua's leadership. With the Deuteronomy 6 Scripture in mind, read what happened to the nation after Joshua died.

READ

Judges 2:6–19

....

⁶ After Joshua had dismissed the Israelites, they went to take possession of the land, each to their own inheritance. ⁷ The people served the Lord throughout the lifetime of Joshua and of the elders who outlived him and who had seen all the great things the Lord had done for Israel.

⁸ Joshua son of Nun, the servant of the Lord, died at the age of a hundred and ten. ⁹ And they buried him in the land of his inheritance, at Timnath Heres in the hill country of Ephraim, north of Mount Gaash.

¹⁰ After that whole generation had been gathered to their ancestors, another generation grew up who knew neither the Lord nor what he had done for Israel. ¹¹ Then the Israelites did evil in the eyes of the Lord and served the Baals. ¹² They forsook the Lord, the God of their ancestors, who had brought them out of Egypt. They followed and worshiped various gods of the peoples around them. They aroused the Lord's anger ¹³ because they forsook him and served Baal and the Ashtoreths. ¹⁴ In his anger against Israel the Lord gave them into the hands of raiders who plundered them. He sold them into the hands of their enemies all around, whom they were no longer able to resist. ¹⁵ Whenever Israel went out to fight, the hand of the Lord was against them to defeat them, just as he had sworn to them. They were in great distress.

¹⁶ Then the Lord raised up judges, who saved them out of the hands of these raiders. ¹⁷ Yet they would not listen to their judges but prostituted themselves to other gods and worshiped them. They quickly turned from the ways of their ancestors, who had been obedient to the Lord's

commands. [18] Whenever the Lord raised up a judge for them, he was with the judge and saved them out of the hands of their enemies as long as the judge lived; for the Lord relented because of their groaning under those who oppressed and afflicted them. [19] But when the judge died, the people returned to ways even more corrupt than those of their ancestors, following other gods and serving and worshiping them. They refused to give up their evil practices and stubborn ways.

What happened in the generations after Israel's leader, Joshua, died?

Compare Deuteronomy 6:12 to Judges 2:10. How had Israel failed to heed God's warning?

How is God's mercy evident in the time of Judges?

Judges 21:25 summarizes this time in Israel's history: "In those days Israel had no king; everyone did as he saw fit." What similarities do you see between our current world and this description of the time of the judges?

In the midst of a dark and broken world, God is still at work to redeem His people because His love and mercy endure forever. In the Book of Ruth, we see God's work of redemption in the time of Judges through one ordinary family.

READ
Ruth 1:1–5

....

[1] In the days when the judges ruled, there was a famine in the land. So a man from Bethlehem in Judah, together with his wife and two sons, went to live for a while in the country of Moab. [2] The man's name was Elimelek, his wife's name was Naomi, and the names of his two sons were Mahlon and Kilion. They were Ephrathites from Bethlehem, Judah. And they went to Moab and lived there.

[3] Now Elimelek, Naomi's husband, died, and she was left with her two sons. [4] They married Moabite women, one named Orpah and the other Ruth. After they had lived there about ten years, [5] both Mahlon and Kilion also died, and Naomi was left without her two sons and her husband.

Who are the characters listed? Draw their family tree. (*See Ruth 4:10 to learn which son Ruth married*).

According to verses 1 and 2, where were Elimelech and his family from? Why might this be important to know?

> See the map in the appendix to enhance your understanding of the location of Israel and Moab

According to verse 1, what challenge was occurring at this time in Israel?

Where did the family travel to?

This family chose to leave God's promised land in the midst of a trial. What is significant about this?

When problems arise in your life, do you naturally go towards God or away from God? Why?

....
....
....
....
....
....
....
....
....

What happened to Naomi's family in Moab in verses 3–5?

....
....
....
....
....
....
....
....
....

What was the family's intention when they first left Bethlehem, and how long did they end up living in Moab?

What did Naomi gain from her time there? What did she lose?

In this moment of Naomi's life, she feels like all hope is lost. We, as readers, can feel her pain and sorrow as we share in her deep mourning. However, Naomi has yet to realize that God still has a good plan for her that is beyond her imagination.

READ

Micah 5:2, 4

---

² "But you, Bethlehem Ephrathah,
though you are small among the clans of Judah,
out of you will come for me
one who will be ruler over Israel,
whose origins are from of old,
from ancient times."

⁴ He will stand and shepherd his flock
in the strength of the Lord,
in the majesty of the name of the Lord his God.
And they will live securely, for then his greatness
will reach to the ends of the earth.

What promises did God make to the Ephrathahites, the small clan Naomi is from?

What events happened in Bethlehem that could fulfill these promises? *(See 1 Samuel 16:1, 11–13 and Luke 2:1–7)*

How do these promises from God give you hope for the future?

Think about your own life story. Write down a little bit of your own family history, where you come from, who is in your life, and where you are now.

Looking back on your life, where do you see God at work even in the most challenging times?

Pray this week the words of King David in Psalm 27.

Psalm 27:13–14.

[13] I remain confident of this:
I will see the goodness of the Lord
in the land of the living.
[14] Wait for the Lord;
be strong and take heart
and wait for the Lord.
Amen.

WEEK 2 ADDITIONAL SCRIPTURE

Ruth 4:10a

¹⁰ I have also acquired Ruth the Moabite, Mahlon's widow,

1 Samuel 16:1,11–13

¹ The Lord said to Samuel, "How long will you mourn for Saul, since I have rejected him as king over Israel? Fill your horn with oil and be on your way; I am sending you to Jesse of Bethlehem. I have chosen one of his sons to be king."

¹¹ So he asked Jesse, "Are these all the sons you have?"

"There is still the youngest," Jesse answered. "He is tending the sheep."

Samuel said, "Send for him; we will not sit down until he arrives."

¹² So he sent for him and had him brought in. He was glowing with health and had a fine appearance and handsome features.

Then the Lord said, "Rise and anoint him; this is the one."

¹³ So Samuel took the horn of oil and anointed him in the presence of his brothers, and from that day on the Spirit of the Lord came powerfully upon David. Samuel then went to Ramah.

Luke 2:1-7

[1] In those days Caesar Augustus issued a decree that a census should be taken of the entire Roman world. [2] (This was the first census that took place while Quirinius was governor of Syria.) [3] And everyone went to their own town to register.

[4] So Joseph also went up from the town of Nazareth in Galilee to Judea, to Bethlehem the town of David, because he belonged to the house and line of David. [5] He went there to register with Mary, who was pledged to be married to him and was expecting a child. [6] While they were there, the time came for the baby to be born, [7] and she gave birth to her firstborn, a son. She wrapped him in cloths and placed him in a manger, because there was no guest room available for them.

Play the teaching video for Week Two. Use the NOTES page to take notes on anything that stands out to you.
See page 8 for video access instructions.

NOTES

Week 3

THE RETURN HOME

Last week, you were introduced to the characters, and the problem of the story became apparent. Ruth the Moabite married into an Israelite family but was widowed without a child. With no heir to pass on the family name, Ruth wasn't connected by blood to the Israelite family she married into. She was only seen as a Moabite woman. In this week's Scripture, you will get to know the personalities of Noami and Ruth better through their conversations. While Naomi's bitter attitude toward the reality that they face causes her daughters-in-law to question their future, Ruth's loyal and determined personality begins to shine.

As you read the conversations between Naomi and her two daughters-in-law this week, think about if you were traveling the road with these women. Behind you lies the familiar, comfortable way of life; ahead of you stretches the path toward a life of faith, depending not on yourself but on God. The journey with God is filled with possibilities and challenges that push you beyond your comfort zone. Choosing the path toward God means letting go of control and allowing Him to guide you. Which direction will you choose?

Spend time this week reading through the provided Scripture and answering the coinciding questions. Enjoy your quiet time in the Scriptures. When you gather as a group, discuss the questions. Share with each other what you are learning. Savor the discussion around "The Table." Once you have discussed all the questions, watch the teaching video for Week 3.

LEARN

This week, we encounter Naomi and her two Moabite daughters-in-law, Ruth and Orpah, as they journey back to Bethlehem. While on the road, as they are about to enter the promised land, Naomi has a conversation with Ruth and Orpah that brings them to a crossroads in their lives. They must decide if they will return to what is comfortable and familiar in Moab or if they will trust God with the unknown in Israel.

READ

Highlight every use of the word or phrase 'return' and 'go back' in the following Ruth passage.

Ruth 1:6–22

....

⁶ When Naomi heard in Moab that the Lord had come to the aid of his people by providing food for them, she and her daughters-in-law prepared to return home from there. ⁷ With her two daughters-in-law she left the place where she had been living and set out on the road that would take them back to the land of Judah.

⁸ Then Naomi said to her two daughters-in-law, "Go back, each of you, to your mother's home. May the Lord show you kindness, as you have shown kindness to your dead husbands and to me. ⁹ May the Lord grant that each of you will find rest in the home of another husband."

Then she kissed them goodbye and they wept aloud ¹⁰ and said to her, "We will go back with you to your people."

¹¹ But Naomi said, "Return home, my daughters. Why would you come with me? Am I going to have any more sons, who could become your husbands? ¹² Return home, my daughters; I am too old to have another husband. Even if I thought there was still hope for me—even if I had a husband tonight and then gave birth to sons—¹³ would you wait until they grew up? Would you remain unmarried for them? No, my daughters. It is more bitter for me than for you, because the Lord's hand has turned against me!"

¹⁴ At this they wept aloud again. Then Orpah kissed her mother-in-law goodbye, but Ruth clung to her.

¹⁵ "Look," said Naomi, "your sister-in-law is going back to her people and her gods. Go back with her."

[16] But Ruth replied, "Don't urge me to leave you or to turn back from you. Where you go I will go, and where you stay I will stay. Your people will be my people and your God my God. [17] Where you die I will die, and there I will be buried. May the Lord deal with me, be it ever so severely, if even death separates you and me." [18] When Naomi realized that Ruth was determined to go with her, she stopped urging her.

[19] So the two women went on until they came to Bethlehem. When they arrived in Bethlehem, the whole town was stirred because of them, and the women exclaimed, "Can this be Naomi?"

[20] "Don't call me Naomi," she told them. "Call me Mara, because the Almighty has made my life very bitter. [21] I went away full, but the Lord has brought me back empty. Why call me Naomi? The Lord has afflicted me; the Almighty has brought misfortune upon me."

[22] So Naomi returned from Moab accompanied by Ruth the Moabite, her daughter-in-law, arriving in Bethlehem as the barley harvest was beginning.

Read Deuteronomy 23:3-5 to learn about the history between Moab and Israel.

Deuteronomy 23:3–5

³ No Ammonite or Moabite or any of their descendants may enter the assembly of the LORD, not even in the tenth generation. ⁴ For they did not come to meet you with bread and water on your way when you came out of Egypt, and they hired Balaam son of Beor from Pethor in Aram Naharaim to pronounce a curse on you. ⁵ However, the LORD your God would not listen to Balaam but turned the curse into a blessing for you, because the LORD your God loves you.

According to the Ruth passage, what does Naomi pray that the Lord will do for Ruth and Orpah in verses 8–9?

What does this prayer reveal about Naomi's understanding of God's character?

Where does Naomi encourage Ruth and Orpah to return to?

According to verses 11–13, what does Naomi feel is impossible for Ruth and Orpah in Israel?

Considering Deuteronomy 23, why would it be easier for Naomi if Ruth and Orpah didn't return with her to Israel?

What aspect of Ruth's loyalty stands out to you in verses 16–18?

Who did Ruth the Moabite proclaim faith in?

Who is someone in your life whose faith in the Lord has drawn you to them?

How has your relationship with that person impacted your own faith?

The decision Ruth and Naomi faced, to have faith in God or return to a life without God, is a decision we each face. Why do you think some people think it is easier to choose a life without God?

....

....

....

....

....

....

....

....

....

What does God promise for those who choose Him? If you have a favorite Scripture of God's promise, write it down and share it with your group.

....

....

....

....

....

....

....

....

....

God chose the people of Israel to be the nation through whom He would send the Redeemer of the world. As you read in Week 1, God told Abraham in Genesis 12:3, "all peoples on earth will be blessed through you." This promise of God was to show that Jesus, the Redeemer, would come from the lineage of Abraham to bring salvation to ALL who believe in Him.

READ

Genesis 15:6

....

⁶ Abram believed the Lord, and he credited it to him as righteousness.

Isaiah 61:10–11

....

¹⁰ I delight greatly in the Lord;
my soul rejoices in my God.
For he has clothed me with garments of salvation
and arrayed me in a robe of his righteousness,
as a bridegroom adorns his head like a priest,
and as a bride adorns herself with her jewels.
¹¹ For as the soil makes the sprout come up
and a garden causes seeds to grow,
so the Sovereign Lord will make righteousness
and praise spring up before all nations.

What do these verses reveal about who can be considered righteous and how?

Considering these verses, why do you think the author emphasized that Ruth was a Moabite?

When the women entered Bethlehem, Naomi felt empty, hopeless, and bitter. However, Ruth's newly claimed and bold faith in the Lord was carrying them into a new beginning.

How does it encourage you to know that God used Ruth, someone considered insignificant and an outsider, to exemplify true faith in the Lord?

Pray this week the words of King David in Psalm 23.

PRAY
Psalm 23:1-6 (NKJV)

[1] The LORD is my shepherd;
I shall not want.
[2] He makes me to lie down in green pastures;
He leads me beside the still waters.
[3] He restores my soul;
He leads me in the paths of righteousness
For His name's sake.

[4] Yea, though I walk through the valley of the shadow of death,
I fear no evil;
For You are with me;
Your rod and Your staff, they comfort me.

[5] You prepare a table before me in the presence of my enemies;
You anoint my head with oil;
My cup runs over.
[6] Surely goodness and mercy shall follow me
All the days of my life;
And I will dwell in the house of the LORD
Forever.
AMEN

Think about how these words apply to Ruth and your own life.

Ruth 1:20–21

[20] "Don't call me Naomi," she told them. "Call me Mara, because the Almighty has made my life very bitter. [21] I went away full, but the Lord has brought me back empty. Why call me Naomi? The Lord has afflicted me; the Almighty has brought misfortune upon me."

Play the teaching video for Week Three. Use the NOTES page to take notes on anything that stands out to you.
See page 8 for video access instructions.

NOTES

Week 4
THE GIFT OF HARVEST

Ruth and Naomi arrived in Bethlehem with a bleak outlook on life. Their secure future was ripped away the moment they both became widows. Ruth proclaimed faith in the one true God, but the Israelites didn't see her as a fellow believer but only the fact of where she was born. As a foreigner, only a miracle from God could give her the secure future in Israel that she desperately desired. This week, you will be introduced to a new character in the story: Boaz. After Ruth and Naomi's suffocating time of grief, Boaz was the breath of fresh air that they need.

As you read and study, look for the ways that God was working behind the scenes in Ruth and Naomi's lives. Think of how God works behind the scenes in your own life. How has He cared for you at a time when you were suffocating in grief? When has God revealed Himself to you at a time you needed it most?

Spend time this week reading through the provided Scripture and answering the coinciding questions. Enjoy your quiet time in the Scriptures. When you gather as a group, discuss the questions. Share with each other what you are learning. Savor the discussion around "The Table." Once you have discussed all the questions, watch the teaching video for Week 4.

LEARN

As childless, unprotected, widowed women, Naomi and Ruth find themselves in a vulnerable position in the patriarchal society of ancient Israel. Women at this time didn't have the right to own property or earn a living wage. Their worth was reliant on the men in their lives. Without a husband or a son, Naomi and Ruth were left with nothing. It is hard to wrap our modern minds around the reality that Naomi and Ruth were facing, but it is key to understanding the destitute future that lay before them. Ruth, being a foreigner, is the most susceptible to harm and least likely to be accepted in Israelite culture, but her loyalty, love, and concern for her mother-in-law outweigh any fears she may have. Ruth has set her sights on the harvest that the Lord has provided, and she intends to gather what they need from it.

Ruth 2:1–3

[1] Now Naomi had a relative on her husband's side, a man of standing from the clan of Elimelek, whose name was Boaz.

[2] And Ruth the Moabite said to Naomi, "Let me go to the fields and pick up the leftover grain behind anyone in whose eyes I find favor."

Naomi said to her, "Go ahead, my daughter." [3] So she went out, entered a field and began to glean behind the harvesters. As it turned out, she was working in a field belonging to Boaz, who was from the clan of Elimelek.

What do you learn about Boaz from verse 1?

According to verse 3, how did Ruth end up in Boaz's field?

What does this tell you about how God directs us?

Prior to Israel entering the promised land, God gave them the law. This law provided guidelines for living and included provisions for caring for foreigners, widows, orphans, and anyone in need. God required landowners to make certain provisions for others through their land, specifically their crops. Read the following laws that were in place for the landowners.

READ
Leviticus 23:22

....

²² "'When you reap the harvest of your land, do not reap to the very edges of your field or gather the gleanings of your harvest. Leave them for the poor and for the foreigner residing among you. I am the Lord your God.'"

Deuteronomy 24:19

....

¹⁹ When you are harvesting in your field and you overlook a sheaf, do not go back to get it. Leave it for the foreigner, the fatherless and the widow, so that the LORD your God may bless you in all the work of your hands.

Deuteronomy 10:17–19

....

¹⁷ For the Lord your God is God of gods and Lord of lords, the great God, mighty and awesome, who shows no partiality and accepts no bribes. ¹⁸ He defends the cause of the fatherless and the widow, and loves the foreigner residing among you, giving them food and clothing. ¹⁹ And you are to love those who are foreigners, for you yourselves were foreigners in Egypt.

In a harvest, the reapers were Israelite workers who were hired to work for pay.* The reapers would gather and bundle the grain to be used or sold. The gleaners would follow behind the reapers, picking up any grain left behind in the field.

What restrictions did God give Israel that would allow someone like Ruth to glean in a field?

What do these Scriptures teach you about God's care and provision for those in need?

---

* Dr. Thomas L. Constable, "Notes on Ruth," 2024 Edition, soniclight.com, p. 29.

How can you apply this same principle in your life today?

....

....

....

....

....

READ

Ruth 2:4-17

....

⁴ Just then Boaz arrived from Bethlehem and greeted the harvesters, "The Lord be with you!"

"The Lord bless you!" they answered.

⁵ Boaz asked the overseer of his harvesters, "Who does that young woman belong to?"

⁶ The overseer replied, "She is the Moabite who came back from Moab with Naomi. ⁷ She said, 'Please let me glean and gather among the sheaves behind the harvesters.' She came into the field and has remained here from morning till now, except for a short rest in the shelter."

⁸ So Boaz said to Ruth, "My daughter, listen to me. Don't go and glean in another field and don't go away from here. Stay here with the women who work for me. ⁹ Watch the field where the men are harvesting, and

follow along after the women. I have told the men not to lay a hand on you. And whenever you are thirsty, go and get a drink from the water jars the men have filled."

[10] At this, she bowed down with her face to the ground. She asked him, "Why have I found such favor in your eyes that you notice me—a foreigner?"

[11] Boaz replied, "I've been told all about what you have done for your mother-in-law since the death of your husband—how you left your father and mother and your homeland and came to live with a people you did not know before. [12] May the Lord repay you for what you have done. May you be richly rewarded by the Lord, the God of Israel, under whose wings you have come to take refuge."

[13] "May I continue to find favor in your eyes, my lord," she said. "You have put me at ease by speaking kindly to your servant—though I do not have the standing of one of your servants."

[14] At mealtime Boaz said to her, "Come over here. Have some bread and dip it in the wine vinegar."

When she sat down with the harvesters, he offered her some roasted grain. She ate all she wanted and had some left over. [15] As she got up to glean, Boaz gave orders to his men, "Let her gather among the sheaves and don't reprimand her. [16] Even pull out some stalks for her from the bundles and leave them for her to pick up, and don't rebuke her."

[17] So Ruth gleaned in the field until evening. Then she threshed the barley she had gathered, and it amounted to about an ephah.

In reading these Scriptures, what stands out to you about Boaz? (His character, how he interacts with his field workers, how he interacts with Ruth, etc.)

....
....
....
....
....
....
....
....
....

List all the ways Boaz provides for Ruth.

....
....
....
....
....
....
....
....
....

What do you learn about Boaz's care for Ruth as a whole person beyond just meeting her physical needs?

According to verse 10, how did Ruth react to Boaz's kindness?

What does this reveal about how Ruth thought she would be treated as a Moabite gleaning in the field?

....

....

....

....

....

....

....

An ephah is estimated to weigh around 30 pounds of grain and was an unfathomably generous amount for one day of gleaning.* When have you received an abundance of kindness you didn't expect?

....

....

....

....

....

....

....

....

....

....

_____

* John F. Walvoord and Roy B. Zuck, *The Bible Knowledge Commentary: An Exposition of the Scriptures.* (Wheaton, IL: Victor Books, 1985).

You can imagine Ruth beaming with joy as she staggered home under the load of barley she carried to Naomi. Not only is she bringing with her the barley that she gleaned but also the stories of unexpected kindness shown to her by Boaz.

READ
Ruth 2:18–23

[18] She carried it back to town, and her mother-in-law saw how much she had gathered. Ruth also brought out and gave her what she had left over after she had eaten enough.

[19] Her mother-in-law asked her, "Where did you glean today? Where did you work? Blessed be the man who took notice of you!"

Then Ruth told her mother-in-law about the one at whose place she had been working. "The name of the man I worked with today is Boaz," she said.

[20] "The LORD bless him!" Naomi said to her daughter-in-law. "He has not stopped showing his kindness to the living and the dead." She added, "That man is our close relative; he is one of our guardian-redeemers."

[21] Then Ruth the Moabite said, "He even said to me, 'Stay with my workers until they finish harvesting all my grain.'"

[22] Naomi said to Ruth her daughter-in-law, "It will be good for you, my daughter, to go with the women who work for him, because in someone else's field you might be harmed."

[23] So Ruth stayed close to the women of Boaz to glean until the barley and wheat harvests were finished. And she lived with her mother-in-law.

What stands out to you in Naomi's reaction to Ruth's return from her day of gleaning?

....
....
....
....
....
....
....
....
....
....

Compare verse 20 to Ruth 1:20–21. What differences do you notice in how Naomi speaks of the Lord now compared to when she first arrived in Bethlehem?

....
....
....
....
....
....
....
....
....

How do you see the Lord turning Naomi's grief into hope?

....

....

....

....

....

....

....

Psalm 34:8 says, "Taste and see that the LORD is good." God's provision granted Ruth safety in the field and a place at Boaz's table. Naomi sees the provision of grain as a light shining in the darkness, giving her fresh eyes to the Lord's kindness. Although the problem of no husband and no son for Ruth is still looming, these small provisions give the women a taste that the Lord is indeed good.

What challenges are you facing? What small provisions have you received that remind you the Lord is good, even in the midst of those challenges?

....

....

....

....

....

....

....

Pray this week the words of King David in Psalm 34.

PRAY

Psalm 34:1-8

---

¹ I will extol the LORD at all times;
his praise will always be on my lips.
² I will glory in the LORD;
let the afflicted hear and rejoice.
³ Glorify the LORD with me;
let us exalt his name together.

⁴ I sought the LORD, and he answered me;
he delivered me from all my fears.
⁵ Those who look to him are radiant;
their faces are never covered with shame.
⁶ This poor man called, and the LORD heard him;
he saved him out of all his troubles.
⁷ The angel of the LORD encamps around those who fear
him,
and he delivers them.

⁸ Taste and see that the LORD is good;
blessed is the one who takes refuge in him.
AMEN

WEEK 4 ADDITIONAL SCRIPTURE

Ruth 1:20–21

[20] "Don't call me Naomi," she told them. "Call me Mara, because the Almighty has made my life very bitter. [21] I went away full, but the LORD has brought me back empty. Why call me Naomi? The LORD has afflicted me; the Almighty has brought misfortune upon me."

Play the teaching video for Week Four. Use the NOTES page to take notes on anything that stands out to you.
See page 8 for video access instructions.

NOTES

Week 5

PATH TO REDEMPTION

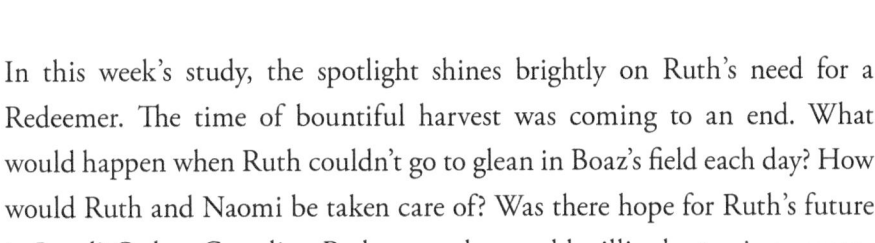

In this week's study, the spotlight shines brightly on Ruth's need for a Redeemer. The time of bountiful harvest was coming to an end. What would happen when Ruth couldn't go to glean in Boaz's field each day? How would Ruth and Naomi be taken care of? Was there hope for Ruth's future in Israel? Only a Guardian-Redeemer who would willingly step in to marry Ruth could secure the future that she longed for.

As you read this week's passage, consider how you plan for your future. Who do you involve while you discuss options for your plans? How might you begin seeking God while you plan, hope, and dream for the future?

Spend time this week reading through the provided Scripture and answering the coinciding questions. Enjoy your quiet time in the Scripture. When you gather as a group, discuss the questions. Share with each other what you are learning. Savor the discussion around "The Table." Once you have discussed all the questions, watch the teaching video for Week 5.

LEARN

Ruth chapter 3 takes us to a scene where Boaz and his workers are winnowing barley on the threshing floor. Winnowing the grain is one of the final steps of the harvest. The eminent end to the harvest causes Naomi to wonder what is next for her and Ruth. Boaz's field provided the temporary provision of grain and safety throughout the harvest, but what about a lasting provision for a family and descendant? Naomi devises a plan, and we will see God step into her human-designed plan to ensure His love and redemption provide the ultimate way forward.

READ
Ruth 3:1–6

¹ One day Ruth's mother-in-law Naomi said to her, "My daughter, I must find a home for you, where you will be well provided for. ² Now Boaz, with whose women you have worked, is a relative of ours. Tonight he will be winnowing barley on the threshing floor. ³ Wash, put on perfume, and get dressed in your best clothes. Then go down to the threshing floor, but don't let him know you are there until he has finished eating and drinking. ⁴ When he lies down, note the place where he is lying. Then go and uncover his feet and lie down. He will tell you what to do."

⁵ "I will do whatever you say," Ruth answered. ⁶ So she went down to the threshing floor and did everything her mother-in-law told her to do.

What is Naomi's plan for Ruth? List every step of her plan.

What do you think Naomi's motives are for this plan?

....
....
....
....
....
....
....
....
....

What does Ruth's obedience tell you about her?

....
....
....
....
....
....
....
....
....
....

READ
Ruth 3:7–18

....

7 When Boaz had finished eating and drinking and was in good spirits, he went over to lie down at the far end of the grain pile. Ruth approached quietly, uncovered his feet and lay down. 8 In the middle of the night something startled the man; he turned—and there was a woman lying at his feet!

9 "Who are you?" he asked.

"I am your servant Ruth," she said. "Spread the corner of your garment over me, since you are a guardian-redeemer of our family."

10 "The Lord bless you, my daughter," he replied. "This kindness is greater than that which you showed earlier: You have not run after the younger men, whether rich or poor. 11 And now, my daughter, don't be afraid. I will do for you all you ask. All the people of my town know that you are a woman of noble character. 12 Although it is true that I am a guardian-redeemer of our family, there is another who is more closely related than I. 13 Stay here for the night, and in the morning if he wants to do his duty as your guardian-redeemer, good; let him redeem you. But if he is not willing, as surely as the Lord lives I will do it. Lie here until morning."

14 So she lay at his feet until morning, but got up before anyone could be recognized; and he said, "No one must know that a woman came to the threshing floor."

¹⁵ He also said, "Bring me the shawl you are wearing and hold it out." When she did so, he poured into it six measures of barley and placed the bundle on her. Then he went back to town.

¹⁶ When Ruth came to her mother-in-law, Naomi asked, "How did it go, my daughter?"

Then she told her everything Boaz had done for her ¹⁷ and added, "He gave me these six measures of barley, saying, 'Don't go back to your mother-in-law empty-handed.'"

¹⁸ Then Naomi said, "Wait, my daughter, until you find out what happens. For the man will not rest until the matter is settled today."

Ruth uncovering Boaz's feet and asking him to spread a garment over her sounds peculiar, especially regarding a marriage proposal. Although this interaction may be confusing, this passage shows that God gave Ruth the desire to enter into a covenant marriage relationship with Boaz. She is asking Boaz to be the one through whom she finds refuge and the one through whom she is redeemed.

Look back at Ruth 2:12. What did Boaz pray for Ruth?

How is Ruth's request for Boaz to be her guardian-redeemer an answer to that prayer?

The word "kindness" in verse 10 is a translation of the Hebrew word "hesed," which is used elsewhere in Scripture to describe the Lord's abounding loyal love. How has Ruth shown loyal love to Naomi and Boaz?

Considering verse 11, what characteristics make someone of noble character?

....

....

....

....

....

....

....

....

....

Which aspect of Ruth's loyal love and noble character do you desire to put into action in your life?

....

....

....

....

....

....

....

....

....

In verses 9–13, the term "guardian-redeemer" is used three different times.
What does a guardian do for someone?

What does a redeemer do for someone?

What do you think someone who is both a guardian and redeemer would do?

....

....

....

....

....

....

....

....

This Scripture describes the law put in place to protect and carry on the family line in Israel. Boaz is a relative but not a brother-in-law of Ruth. Ruth is asking Boaz to step in as a substitute and be the one to redeem their family, even though he is not obligated to do so.

What might Boaz be sacrificing in his own life to be the guardian-redeemer of Ruth?

....

....

....

....

....

....

....

Deuteronomy 25:5–6: (NET)

5 If brothers live together and one of them dies without having a son, the dead man's wife must not remarry someone outside the family. Instead, her late husband's brother must go to her, marry her, and perform the duty of a brother-in-law. 6 Then the first son she bears will continue the name of the dead brother, thus preventing his name from being blotted out of Israel.

Considering this context, what stands out to you about Boaz's response to Ruth in Ruth 3:10–15?

What could keep Boaz from being the one to redeem Ruth?

How does Boaz demonstrate his determination and willingness to be the redeemer?

....

....

....

....

....

....

....

....

....

....

....

We, like Ruth, need to be redeemed. We are each born with a sinful nature due to the consequences of living in a broken world. The penalty of sin is separation from God. We desperately need a guardian-redeemer to pay the price for our sins and give us the restoration needed to bring us back to God. The good news is that instead of us searching for the guardian-redeemer who could pay the redemption price, God chose the One and sent the One True Guardian-Redeemer. There is only one who could redeem our brokenness, only one who could be the substitute for the punishment we deserve. Jesus, The Son of God, sacrificed Himself so that He could step in as our guardian-redeemer. Jesus came to earth, both fully human and fully God, to pay the price for our sins once and for all.

READ
1 Peter 1:18–19

....

[18] For you know that it was not with perishable things such as silver or gold that you were redeemed from the empty way of life handed down to you from your ancestors, [19] but with the precious blood of Christ, a lamb without blemish or defect.

Romans 6:22–23

....

[22] But now that you have been set free from sin and have become slaves of God, the benefit you reap leads to holiness, and the result is eternal life. [23] For the wages of sin is death, but the gift of God is eternal life in Christ Jesus our Lord.

Ephesians 1:7–10

....

[7] In him we have redemption through his blood, the forgiveness of sins, in accordance with the riches of God's grace [8] that he lavished on us. With all wisdom and understanding, [9] he made known to us the mystery of his will according to his good pleasure, which he purposed in Christ, [10] to be put into effect when the times reach their fulfillment— to bring unity to all things in heaven and on earth under Christ.

Ephesians 2:12-13

....

¹² remember that at that time you were separate from Christ, excluded from citizenship in Israel and foreigners to the covenants of the promise, without hope and without God in the world. ¹³ But now in Christ Jesus you who once were far away have been brought near by the blood of Christ.

What stands out to you most in these passages about redemption and why?

What does redemption through Christ Jesus mean to you personally?

How does knowing that God loves you enough to send you a guardian-re-deemer make you feel?

Pray this week the words of King David in Psalm 51.

Psalm 51:1–12.

....

[1] Have mercy on me, O God,
according to your unfailing love;
according to your great compassion
blot out my transgressions.
[2] Wash away all my iniquity
and cleanse me from my sin.

[3] For I know my transgressions,
and my sin is always before me.
[4] Against you, you only, have I sinned
and done what is evil in your sight;
so you are right in your verdict
and justified when you judge.
[5] Surely I was sinful at birth,
sinful from the time my mother conceived me.
[6] Yet you desired faithfulness even in the womb;
you taught me wisdom in that secret place.

[7] Cleanse me with hyssop, and I will be clean;
wash me, and I will be whiter than snow.
[8] Let me hear joy and gladness;
let the bones you have crushed rejoice.
[9] Hide your face from my sins
and blot out all my iniquity.

¹⁰ Create in me a pure heart, O God,

and renew a steadfast spirit within me.

¹¹ Do not cast me from your presence

or take your Holy Spirit from me.

¹² Restore to me the joy of your salvation

and grant me a willing spirit, to sustain me.

AMEN

WEEK 5 ADDITIONAL SCRIPTURE

Ruth 2:12 (NASB)

¹² "May the LORD reward your work, and may your wages be full from the LORD, the God of Israel, under whose wings you have come to take refuge."

Play the teaching video for Week Five. Use the NOTES page to take notes on anything that stands out to you.

See page 8 for video access instructions.

NOTES

Week 6

THE REDEEMER REVEALED

Last week, Ruth approached Boaz to ask if he would be her guardian-redeemer. You also examined Scripture that reveals Jesus as the guardian-redeemer for each of us. Unlike Ruth, we don't have to search for the one who can redeem us. God has shown that Jesus is the only redeemer we need. Boaz is a beautiful reflection of Jesus in the Old Testament. This week you will watch Boaz as he stops at nothing to ensure that Ruth is redeemed.

As you study this week, carefully examine Boaz's actions. How does Boaz's determination and care for Ruth remind you of how Jesus cares for and loves you?

Spend time this week reading through the provided Scripture and answering the coinciding questions. Enjoy your quiet time in the Scriptures and get to know the Redeemer. When you gather as a group, discuss the questions. Share with each other what you are learning. Savor the discussion around "The Table." Once you have discussed all the questions, watch the teaching video for Week 6.

LEARN

In Ruth chapter 4, Boaz takes action. You will also revisit the passage from Deuteronomy 25 you read last week. Compare Boaz's actions to the law set in place. The setting of this chapter is the town gate, the typical place for official business transactions in ancient cities like Bethlehem. The conversations and negotiations that you read are to determine who would redeem the land of Elimelech and also who would redeem the widows that Elimelech and his sons have left behind. This conversation has many details, but the ultimate purpose is determining whom God has chosen to be Ruth's guardian-redeemer.

READ
Deuteronomy 25:5–10 (NET)

....

[5] If brothers live together and one of them dies without having a son, the dead man's wife must not remarry someone outside the family. Instead, her late husband's brother must go to her, marry her, and perform the duty of a brother-in-law. [6] Then the first son she bears will continue the name of the dead brother, thus preventing his name from being blotted out of Israel. [7] But if the man does not want to marry his brother's widow, then she must go to the elders at the town gate and say, "My husband's brother refuses to preserve his brother's name in Israel; he is unwilling to perform the duty of a brother-in-law to me!" [8] Then the elders of his city must summon him and speak to him. If he persists, saying, "I don't want to marry her," [9] then his sister-in-law must approach him in view of the elders, remove his sandal from his foot, and spit in his face. She will then respond, "Thus may it be done to any man who does not maintain his brother's family line!" [10] His family name will be referred to in Israel as "the family of the one whose sandal was removed."

Ruth 4:1–10

....

[1] Meanwhile Boaz went up to the town gate and sat down there just as the guardian-redeemer he had mentioned came along. Boaz said, "Come over here, my friend, and sit down." So he went over and sat down.

² Boaz took ten of the elders of the town and said, "Sit here," and they did so. ³ Then he said to the guardian-redeemer, "Naomi, who has come back from Moab, is selling the piece of land that belonged to our relative Elimelek. ⁴ I thought I should bring the matter to your attention and suggest that you buy it in the presence of these seated here and in the presence of the elders of my people. If you will redeem it, do so. But if you will not, tell me, so I will know. For no one has the right to do it except you, and I am next in line."

"I will redeem it," he said.

⁵ Then Boaz said, "On the day you buy the land from Naomi, you also acquire Ruth the Moabite, the dead man's widow, in order to maintain the name of the dead with his property."

⁶ At this, the guardian-redeemer said, "Then I cannot redeem it because I might endanger my own estate. You redeem it yourself. I cannot do it."

⁷ (Now in earlier times in Israel, for the redemption and transfer of property to become final, one party took off his sandal and gave it to the other. This was the method of legalizing transactions in Israel.)

⁸ So the guardian-redeemer said to Boaz, "Buy it yourself." And he removed his sandal.

⁹ Then Boaz announced to the elders and all the people, "Today you are witnesses that I have bought from Naomi all the property of Elimelek, Kilion and Mahlon. ¹⁰ I have also acquired Ruth the Moabite, Mahlon's widow, as my wife, in order to maintain the name of the dead with his property, so that his name will not disappear from among his family or from his hometown. Today you are witnesses!"

What similarities do you see in the Deuteronomy passage with the actions and steps that Boaz takes?

What do you admire about Boaz's actions and respect for the relative with the legal right to redeem Ruth?

Why did the closer relative initially say, "I will redeem it," but then change his mind and say, "I cannot do it?"

....

....

....

....

....

....

....

....

....

In verses 9–10, Boaz announces and makes a declaration. What part of this declaration stands out as significant to you?

....

....

....

....

....

....

....

....

....

Through Boaz's declaration of Ruth as his wife, he was changing her life. Ruth was born a Moabite, a foreigner outside of the covenant that God made to the nation of Israel. As a widow without a descendant, she was without a promised future. In the same way that Ruth couldn't make a way for herself, God revealed that He makes a way and does for us what we can't do on our own. Jesus is the one who came to bring outsiders into God's family and inside God's promises. Ruth needed a guardian-redeemer so that she could be safe, have hope for a future, and be secure in the promises of God Almighty. For Ruth, God chose and provided Boaz to be her guardian-redeemer.

How is Boaz a representation of Jesus our Redeemer?

¹¹ Then the elders and all the people at the gate said, "We are witnesses. May the Lord make the woman who is coming into your home like Rachel and Leah, who together built up the family of Israel. May you have standing in Ephrathah and be famous in Bethlehem. ¹² Through the offspring the Lord gives you by this young woman, may your family be like that of Perez, whom Tamar bore to Judah."

¹³ So Boaz took Ruth and she became his wife. When he made love to her, the Lord enabled her to conceive, and she gave birth to a son. ¹⁴ The women said to Naomi: "Praise be to the Lord, who this day has not left you without a guardian-redeemer. May he become famous throughout Israel! ¹⁵ He will renew your life and sustain you in your old age. For your daughter-in-law, who loves you and who is better to you than seven sons, has given him birth."

¹⁶ Then Naomi took the child in her arms and cared for him. ¹⁷ The women living there said, "Naomi has a son!" And they named him Obed. He was the father of Jesse, the father of David.

Compare and contrast verses 14–17 with Ruth 1:19–22. How are these inter-actions between the women and Naomi different?

What changes do you see in Naomi's circumstances and attitude toward God?

How did God transform Naomi's emptiness and bitterness into a renewed life?

....

....

....

....

....

....

....

....

....

How has God renewed you when you felt empty?

....

....

....

....

....

....

....

....

....

In verses 11–13, what do the elders pray the Lord will do for Ruth and Boaz?

How does this prayer recognize Ruth as a part of the family of God and desire God's promises to be fulfilled through her? (See Micah 5:2, 4.)

How do you see the prayers of the elders answered in verses 13–17?

....

....

....

....

....

....

....

....

....

....

....

....

....

....

....

....

....

....

The Book of Ruth ends with a genealogy. While genealogies can be monotonous to read, they are necessary to connect the story of God's redemptive plan through Scripture.

Ruth 4:17–22

17 The women living there said, "Naomi has a son!" And they named him Obed. He was the father of Jesse, the father of David.

18 This, then, is the family line of Perez:

Perez was the father of Hezron,

19 Hezron the father of Ram,

Ram the father of Amminadab,

20 Amminadab the father of Nahshon,

Nahshon the father of Salmon,

21 Salmon the father of Boaz,

Boaz the father of Obed,

22 Obed the father of Jesse,

and Jesse the father of David.

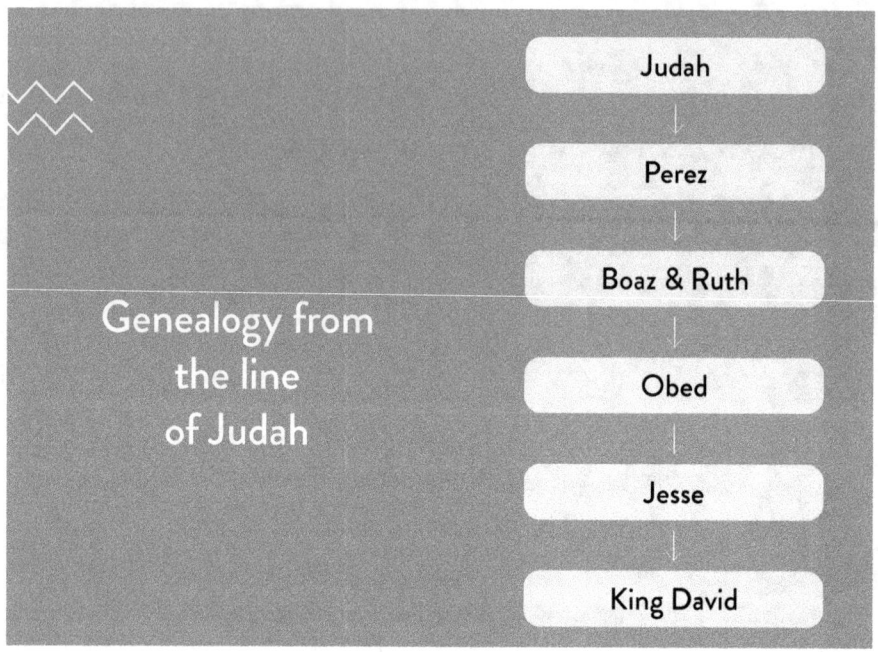

The "main characters" from the family line in Ruth 4:18–22

According to this genealogy, who is a direct descendent of Ruth?

In week 2 of this study, we learned the Book of Ruth was written during the time of Judges in Israel. The author of Judges described that period of time in this way: "In those days Israel had no king; everyone did as they saw fit" (21:25).

What made Kind David a great king? (See 1 Chronicles 18:14, Ezekiel 34:23–24, and 1 Samuel 16:11–13.)

What does it tell you about God that He would send a King for His people through Ruth?

God sent King David to rule over Israel. David was a great king. His life showed that he truly loved God, but he, just like all humans, was imperfect. We can learn from David's heart for God even through his sin. His beautiful prayers throughout the Psalms exude David's trust and reliance on God. God sent David to point forward to the only perfect king, King Jesus. God desires to be King in each and every one of our lives. He sent Jesus to be your Redeemer and to be the everlasting King.

READ
Acts 13:17–23

....

[17] The God of the people of Israel chose our ancestors; he made the people prosper during their stay in Egypt; with mighty power he led them out of that country; [18] for about forty years he endured their conduct in the wilderness; [19] and he overthrew seven nations in Canaan, giving their land to his people as their inheritance. [20] All this took about 450 years.

"After this, God gave them judges until the time of Samuel the prophet. [21] Then the people asked for a king, and he gave them Saul son of Kish, of the tribe of Benjamin, who ruled forty years. [22] After removing Saul, he made David their king. God testified concerning him: 'I have found David son of Jesse, a man after my own heart; he will do everything I want him to do.'

[23] "From this man's descendants God has brought to Israel the Savior Jesus, as he promised.

Isaiah 9:6-7

···

⁶ For to us a child is born,
to us a son is given,
and the government will be on his shoulders.
And he will be called
Wonderful Counselor, Mighty God,
Everlasting Father, Prince of Peace.
⁷ Of the greatness of his government and peace
there will be no end.
He will reign on David's throne
and over his kingdom,
establishing and upholding it
with justice and righteousness
from that time on and forever.
The zeal of the Lord Almighty
will accomplish this.

How does Acts 13:17–23 show you God's fulfillment of His promise throughout history for a King of Israel and Savior of the World?

···

···

···

···

···

···

···

What does Isaiah 9:6–7 verse teach you about Jesus' Kingship?

Do you know and trust that Jesus is your Redeemer and King?

How does trusting Jesus as King of your life affect how you live each day?

Pray this week the words of King David in Psalm 145.

PRAY
Psalm 145:1–13, 21

¹ I will exalt you, my God the King;
I will praise your name for ever and ever.
² Every day I will praise you
and extol your name for ever and ever.

³ Great is the LORD and most worthy of praise;
his greatness no one can fathom.
⁴ One generation commends your works to another;
they tell of your mighty acts.
⁵ They speak of the glorious splendor of your majesty—
and I will meditate on your wonderful works.
⁶ They tell of the power of your awesome works—
and I will proclaim your great deeds.
⁷ They celebrate your abundant goodness
and joyfully sing of your righteousness.

⁸ The LORD is gracious and compassionate,
slow to anger and rich in love.

⁹ The LORD is good to all;
he has compassion on all he has made.
¹⁰ All your works praise you, Lord;
your faithful people extol you.
¹¹ They tell of the glory of your kingdom

and speak of your might,

[12] so that all people may know of your mighty acts
and the glorious splendor of your kingdom.
[13] Your kingdom is an everlasting kingdom,
and your dominion endures through all generations.

[21] My mouth will speak in praise of the LORD.
Let every creature praise his holy name
for ever and ever.
AMEN

WEEK 6 ADDITIONAL SCRIPTURE

Ruth 1:19–22

[19] So the two women went on until they came to Bethlehem. When they arrived in Bethlehem, the whole town was stirred because of them, and the women exclaimed, "Can this be Naomi?"

[20] "Don't call me Naomi," she told them. "Call me Mara, because the Almighty has made my life very bitter. [21] I went away full, but the Lord has brought me back empty. Why call me Naomi? The Lord has afflicted me; the Almighty has brought misfortune upon me."

[22] So Naomi returned from Moab accompanied by Ruth the Moabite, her daughter-in-law, arriving in Bethlehem as the barley harvest was beginning.

Micah 5:2, 4

2 "But you, Bethlehem Ephrathah,
though you are small among the clans of Judah,
out of you will come for me
one who will be ruler over Israel,
whose origins are from of old,
from ancient times."

4 He will stand and shepherd his flock
in the strength of the Lord,
in the majesty of the name of the Lord his God.
And they will live securely, for then his greatness
will reach to the ends of the earth.

1 Chronicles 18:14 (NASB)

14 So David reigned over all Israel; and he administered justice and righteousness for all his people.

Ezekiel 34:23–24

23 I will place over them one shepherd, my servant David, and he will tend them; he will tend them and be their shepherd. 24 I the LORD will be their God, and my servant David will be prince among them. I the LORD have spoken.

1 Samuel 16:11–13

[11] So he asked Jesse, "Are these all the sons you have?"

"There is still the youngest," Jesse answered. "He is tending the sheep."

Samuel said, "Send for him; we will not sit down until he arrives."

[12] So he sent for him and had him brought in. He was glowing with health and had a fine appearance and handsome features.

Then the LORD said, "Rise and anoint him; this is the one."

[13] So Samuel took the horn of oil and anointed him in the presence of his brothers, and from that day on the Spirit of the LORD came powerfully upon David.

Play the teaching video for Week Six. Use the NOTES page to take notes on anything that stands out to you.
See page 8 for video access instructions.

NOTES

Week 7

GOD SENDS THE REDEEMER OF THE WORLD

The ending to Ruth's story was better than she, Naomi, or Boaz could have imagined. Ruth's desperate need for a Redeemer was fulfilled. Boaz stepped in and paid the price for her redemption! Then, God didn't stop there. He blessed them with a son. Can you even imagine the joy as Ruth held Obed in her arms and looked up to praise the Lord for His goodness in her life? Immeasurably more than she could have dreamt of. Ruth wouldn't have known what would come through her son or that she would be the great-grandmother of King David. But God knew because God had big plans of redemption.

This week, you will jump to the first page in the New Testament in Matthew chapter 1 where God revealed His plan to bring Jesus, the Savior, into the world. This lineage is one you won't want to miss. Think about your own life, who came before you, who might come after you. Will you trust God with His plan?

Spend time this week reading through the provided Scripture and answering the coinciding questions. Enjoy your quiet time in the Scriptures and get to know the Redeemer. When you gather as a group, discuss the questions. Share with each other what you are learning. Savor the discussion around "The Table." Once you have discussed all the questions, watch the teaching video for Week 7.

LEARN

Though there is no record of the details of Ruth's life after the Book of Ruth, her legacy lives on! It led to the birth and reign of King David, but God didn't stop His redemption story there. God would carry the redemption of Ruth all the way through to the birth of His son, the Redeemer of the world. Matthew 1 reveals the lineage of Jesus Christ, the Messiah. In this genealogy, we see forty-two generations listed. The genealogy finally comes to an end with the long-awaited Christ child.

READ
Matthew 1:1–17

[1] This is the genealogy of Jesus the Messiah the son of David, the son of Abraham:

[2] Abraham was the father of Isaac,
Isaac the father of Jacob,

Jacob the father of Judah and his brothers,

³ Judah the father of Perez and Zerah, whose mother was Tamar,

Perez the father of Hezron,

Hezron the father of Ram,

⁴ Ram the father of Amminadab,

Amminadab the father of Nahshon,

Nahshon the father of Salmon,

⁵ Salmon the father of Boaz, whose mother was Rahab,

Boaz the father of Obed, whose mother was Ruth,

Obed the father of Jesse,

⁶ and Jesse the father of King David.

David was the father of Solomon, whose mother had been Uriah's wife,

⁷ Solomon the father of Rehoboam,

Rehoboam the father of Abijah,

Abijah the father of Asa,

⁸ Asa the father of Jehoshaphat,

Jehoshaphat the father of Jehoram,

Jehoram the father of Uzziah,

⁹ Uzziah the father of Jotham,

Jotham the father of Ahaz,

Ahaz the father of Hezekiah,

¹⁰ Hezekiah the father of Manasseh,

Manasseh the father of Amon,

Amon the father of Josiah,

¹¹ and Josiah the father of Jeconiah and his brothers at the time of the exile to Babylon.

12 After the exile to Babylon:

Jeconiah was the father of Shealtiel,

Shealtiel the father of Zerubbabel,

13 Zerubbabel the father of Abihud,

Abihud the father of Eliakim,

Eliakim the father of Azor,

14 Azor the father of Zadok,

Zadok the father of Akim,

Akim the father of Elihud,

15 Elihud the father of Eleazar,

Eleazar the father of Matthan,

Matthan the father of Jacob,

16 and Jacob the father of Joseph, the husband of Mary, and Mary was the mother of Jesus who is called the Messiah.

17 Thus there were fourteen generations in all from Abraham to David, fourteen from David to the exile to Babylon, and fourteen from the exile to the Messiah.

According to verse 1, who is Jesus the son of?

In week one, we examined God's promises to Abraham and David. Re-read Genesis 12:1–3 and 2 Samuel 7:8–9, 16. How does Jesus fulfill these promises?

Forty-two fathers are listed in the lineage to Christ, and only five mothers are recorded. According to verse 5, who is Obed's mother?

What does it mean to you to see her name listed as one of the great names in the lineage of the birth of Jesus? What does this teach you about God?

....
....
....
....
....
....
....
....
....

Read through your study and notes, focusing on the main characters of the story: Naomi, Ruth, and Boaz.

What did you learn from Naomi?

....
....
....
....
....
....
....
....
....

What attributes or character qualities of hers stand out to you?

What would you like to remember about Naomi and apply to your life?

What did you learn from Ruth?

....
....
....
....
....
....
....
....
....
....

What attributes or character qualities of hers stand out to you?

....
....
....
....
....
....
....
....
....
....

What would you like to remember about Ruth and apply to your life?

What did you learn from Boaz?

What attributes or character qualities of his stand out to you?

....

....

....

....

....

....

....

....

What would you like to remember about Boaz and apply to your life?

....

....

....

....

....

....

....

....

There is so much to learn from each character in this story. But the main character of the Book of Ruth was the one working behind the scenes the entire time. The Book of Ruth is the story of God's love, faithfulness, and redemption!

What did the Book of Ruth teach you about God?

What attributes of God are evident in the story?

How have you seen God's plan of redemption for you through the story of Ruth?

....

....

....

....

....

....

....

What do you most want to remember and take with you from your study of Ruth?

....

....

....

....

....

....

....

Throughout this study, you have been reading and praying the Psalms of King David. Now, take time to go back through King David's words and use his songs as inspiration to write a prayer for yourself.

Pray this week your words inspired by the Psalms of King David.

Pray

Genesis 12:1–3

[1] The LORD had said to Abram, "Go from your country, your people and your father's household to the land I will show you.
[2] "I will make you into a great nation, and I will bless you; I will make your name great, and you will be a blessing.
[3] I will bless those who bless you, and whoever curses you I will curse; and all peoples on earth will be blessed through you."

2 Samuel 7:8–9, 16

[8] "Now then, tell my servant David, 'This is what the LORD Almighty says: I took you from the pasture, from tending the flock, and appointed you ruler over my people Israel. [9] I have been with you wherever you have gone, and I have cut off all your enemies from before you. Now I will make your name great, like the names of the greatest men on earth.

[16] Your house and your kingdom will endure forever before me; your throne will be established forever.'"

Play the teaching video for Week Seven. Use the NOTES page to take notes on anything that stands out to you.
See page 8 for video access instructions.

NOTES

APPENDIX

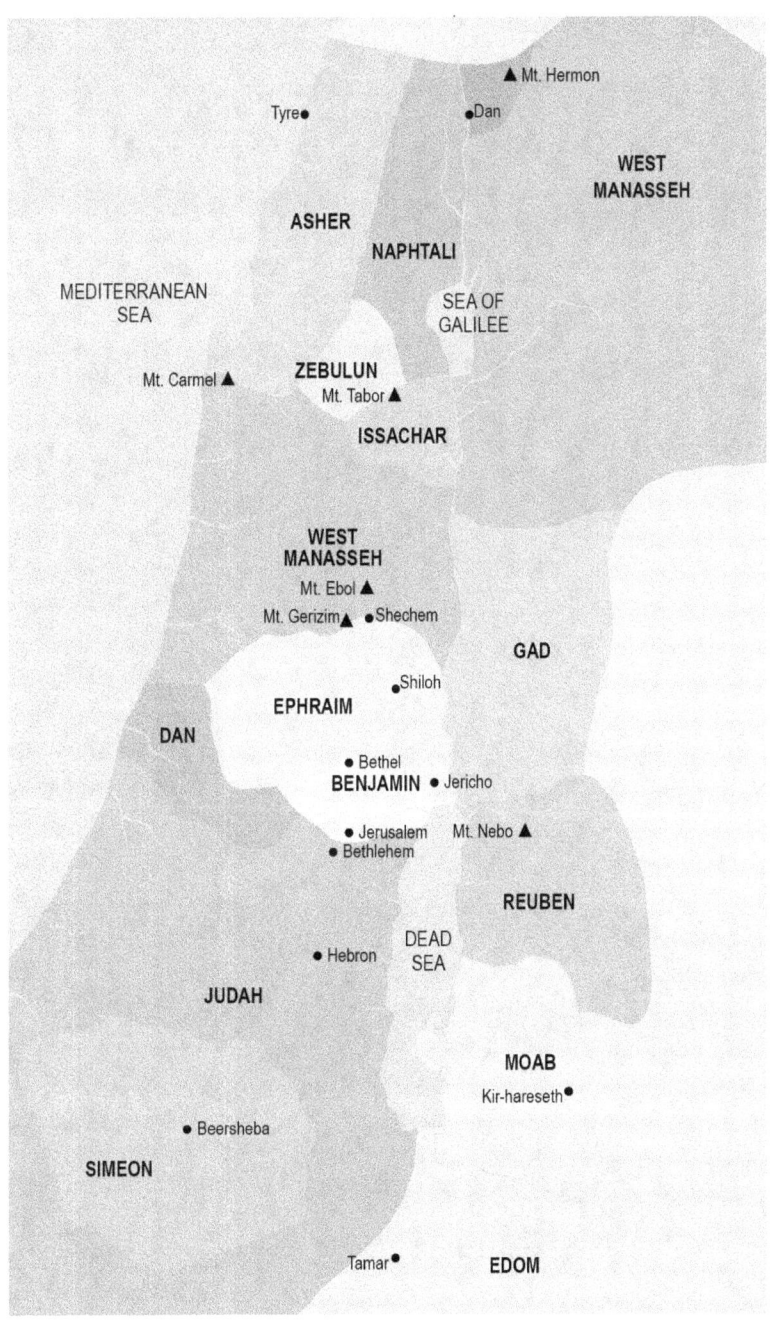

NOTES

NOTES

NOTES

www.ingramcontent.com/pod-product-compliance
Lightning Source LLC
Chambersburg PA
CBHW081659120626
46550CB00010B/2957